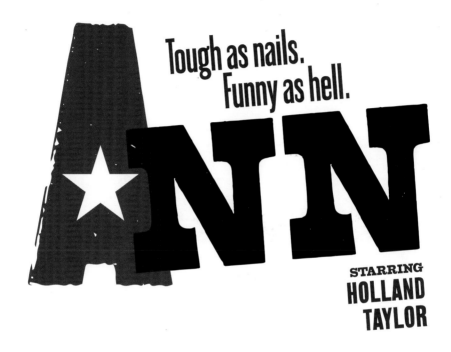

Tough as nails.
Funny as hell.

ANN

STARRING
HOLLAND
TAYLOR

Published by and in support of
The Ann Richards School for Young Women Leaders

FORWARD

My mother, Ann Richards, was larger than life --
passionate, funny, complicated, and determined to
make her mark on the world. Her journey, from an
only child born to hard-scrabble parents in Lakeview,
Texas, to being the first woman elected in her own
right as governor of Texas, had more than its share
of ups and downs. Her personal story, along with her
uncanny humor and plain-spoken truisms, captured the
imagination of the public -- those who knew her and
many more who felt like they did.

In *Ann*, Holland has mastered what many comedians,
politicians, and writers have attempted for years —
she found the voice of Ann Richards. Holland researched
every word, speech, and interview that Ann Richards
ever wrote or spoke. She became a living archive of
Mom's life. Holland's writing and performance tells
her story brilliantly -- as Mother would say, warts and
all. There's not a single word out of place. Books have
been written, documentaries made, but nothing truly
captures the life of my mother like *Ann*.

Mom loved sitting in a dark theater and being
entertained and inspired. I'm grateful that Holland
Taylor has done both with *Ann*. Through Holland's work,
Mom can continue to inspire young women and men, and as
a result some may devote their lives to public service.
She believed there was no higher calling, and nothing
would have pleased her more.

Cecile Richards

— Cecile Richards

A NOTE FROM THE AUTHOR

There is no way to convey my love and appreciation
for the hundred or so friends, associates, and members
of Ann Richards' family who helped me understand her
in a way that would have been utterly impossible
without them.

I was compelled to write this play...the notion to do
it at all, the idea for *how* to write it — its shape and
style — came all in a rush, leaving me wide-eyed with
surprise. And in I plunged. During the darkest hours
of trying to shape a tumultuous mountain of material,
in a daydream I would see Ann in the fifth row, beaming
happily and elbowing our mutual old friend, Liz Smith.
Six years of work later, I have made a journey I could
never have imagined. But I went in whole hog, and
stayed in — working hard and doing the best I could —
which gave me a hint of how I'll bet Ann Richards felt
every single day.

I hope Ann would like this. People loved to please
her...one of her children said to please her was to get
hit with a million suns. So, of course, now I want to
please her, too.

Texans have welcomed me in my endeavor, which I find
incredibly generous (Yankee that I am), and I will
always be grateful for their affection and fun and
open hearts.

As this is a piece of writing based on research, I
should say something about the text itself. I had
intended by now to annotate it, to say who told the
story something was based on, what chunk was cobbled
from this, what sliver was taken from that, and what
large sections were stitched up out of whole cloth,
though based on sure and certain knowledge of my

subject. But, of course, the tide sweeps me along, and I haven't done that yet. (I never did master footnotes in school.)

Most of the play is based on years of overlapping stories told me in significant detail, including fragments of fabulous dialogue, by the players themselves.

The office scenes in the play have been created based on many, many anecdotes and, in some areas, profound and lengthy study — though the play's ending, for obvious reasons, is purely a dream — about someone I do think of now as a friend I know pretty well, and love.

— Holland Taylor

HOLLAND TAYLOR (*Ann Richards and Playwright*). *The New Yorker* has called Holland Taylor "the first vaudeville Gentile we ever saw." Her New York stage performances include Bess in *Breakfast With Les and Bess,* the original productions of *Butley,* opposite Alan Bates, and A.R. Gurney's *The Cocktail Hour*. In Los Angeles she has performed in *Kindertransport* and played opposite Christopher Lloyd in Yasmina Reza's *The Unexpected Man* at the Geffen. She has worked extensively in film and television, appearing in *Romancing the Stone, Jewel of the Nile, To Die For, Next Stop Wonderland, One Fine Day, George of the Jungle, The Truman Show, Happy Accidents, Spy Kids (2* and *3), Keeping the Faith, Legally Blonde* and *Baby Mama,* with Tina Fey and Amy Poehler. On television, Holland has been nominated for an Emmy seven times, winning Best Supporting Actress in a Drama for the sexually popular Judge Roberta Kittleson on "The Practice." Among her numerous series starring roles: "The Powers that Be," Norman Lear's short-lived but highly acclaimed political satire; "Bosom Buddies," with Tom Hanks: and, currently, "Two and a Half Men," with Jon Cryer and Ashton Kutcher. She has performed narrations for the Los Angeles Philharmonic with Esa-Pekka Salonen and John Adams and narrated the *Harry Potter Suite* for John Williams at the Chicago Symphony Orchestra. Holland was a dedicated student of Stella Adler, and has given talks about the work and cultural contribution of this great teacher. Proud to be a Philadelphia native, she went to Westtown Friends School in that area, and took a BA at Bennington

College. In 2005 she became a student again, earning an MA from the University of Santa Monica, and in '07, began work on this play. She will always be grateful to the Galveston Grand Opera's Maureen Patton, who took an enormous "Ann Richards-sized" risk in launching its first run; to Kevin Bailey, our shepherd from the start; to Benjamin Endsley Klein for his promise to "make the vision flesh"; and to Bob Boyett, who read the play as a friend, and looked up from the page as its producer.

Bob Boyett   Harriet Newman Leve

Jane Dubin   Jack Thomas/Mark Johannes and Amy Danis

Sarahbeth Grossman   Jon Cryer/Lisa Joyner   Minerva Productions   Lary Brandt/Brian Dorsey

Kate Hathaway/Allison Thomas   Jennifer Isaacson   Kevin Bailey

IN ASSOCIATION WITH
Lincoln Center Theater

PRESENT

Holland Taylor

IN

ANN

SCENIC DESIGNER	COSTUME DESIGNER	LIGHTING DESIGNER	SOUND DESIGNER	PROJECTION DESIGNER
Michael Fagin	Julie Weiss	Matthew Richards	Ken Huncovsky	Zachary Borovay

WIG DESIGNER	PRESS REPRESENTATIVE	PRODUCTION MANAGER	PRODUCTION STAGE MANAGER
Paul Huntley	The Hartman Group	Peter Fulbright	J. P. Elins

MARKETING	ADVERTISING	GENERAL MANAGEMENT
Leanne Schanzer Promotions, Inc.	SpotCo	101 Productions, Ltd.

ASSOCIATE PRODUCERS

Colleen Barrett   Francesca Zambello and Faith Gay   Nancy T. Beren/Patrick Terry

Marcy Adelman/Paula Kaminsky Davis   Campbell Spencer/Gasparian Suisman   Bonnie Levinson

WRITTEN BY
Holland Taylor

DIRECTED BY
Benjamin Endsley Klein

ANN

By

Holland Taylor

Based on writings of Ann Richards, interviews with her staff,
friends and family, film records, news publications, anecdote,
and imagination.

At first glance the setting is a modest 1930's college
auditorium prepared for a graduation. Flags hang in
the shadows. On the right side of the stage, in golden
light, is an old fashioned carved wood podium. The rich
red curtain backdrop across the proscenium is festooned
with handsome school banners flanking an old pull-down
movie screen, which hangs a man's height above the
stage. Projected on the screen is an old bordered school
banner, which reads: "The Graduating Class welcomes
Governor Ann Richards."

*The lights have dimmed
halfway. As the actual
audience quiets down, the
imaginary college's audience
is heard, an expectant
murmur...*
*The projection of the school
banner is replaced with the
TV news footage of the 1988
Convention-- crowd noises, the
blue background, the huge DNC
logo, the high blue podium,
and Ann Richards is opening
her keynote speech. A long
shot shows the deep volume of
the hall. She repeats "thank
you," smiling broadly, as the
roaring audience quiets down.*

ANN

Good evening ladies and gentlemen. Buenos Noches, Mis
Amigos. *(Huge roar from the crowd, we see several
angles of this, bouncing signs, smiling faces)* Twelve
years ago, Barbara Jordan - another Texas woman-
(applause)- Barbara made the Keynote address to this

convention- and two women in a hundred and sixty years
is about par for the course. But if you give us a
chance, we can perform. After all, Ginger Rogers did
everything that Fred Astaire did, she just did it
backwards and in hi-i-gh heels!

> *The "tape" escapes the confines
> of the screen, "Chariots of
> Fire" sounds, the confetti
> illusion over the convention
> image spreads out over the
> entire proscenium and red
> curtain, through the center
> of which Ann will enter. The
> "tape's" applause continues as
> the curtain lifts. 'Chariots'
> up full, as if played by
> the College. ANN walks on
> unceremoniously, with her blue
> speech box. She waves a "oh,
> c'mon now," and sends up a
> special grin for the music.*

ANN

Thank you. Thank you very much. (*Looking up to the
spot...*) How great you guys put on that music!.. You
know, we used that in every campaign of mine! I never
tired of it-- I would even play it on a little tape
recorder and ear phones on the Hike and Bike trail,
and it always chuffed me up! And my Lord, it sure does
take me back to see a bit of that keynote speech that
changed my life forever...

Look at you, y'all cleaned up pretty well.

I bet some o' you just remember ME 'cause of my _hair_. You know, I notice most of you guys who tease me about my hair don't have any.

I thank you for inviting me to speak at your graduation... I am glad to be here- to help swing the doors wide as you take wing to a new time in your life--

Now, before I go any further, I should probably mention, since you could be from all over the country, you might think I was the first female Governor of Texas, so I want to rush to disabuse you of that notion. Texas elected its first female governor way back in the 1920's. Her name was Ma Fergusson. Ma was called Ma, 'cause she was married to a man named...(_Audience responds- "Pa!"_) This is a pretty sharp crowd.
And Pa was the Governor of Texas. He was impeached for selling pardons to people in the penitentiary, and when they carted Pa off to the Pen himself, Ma was elected in his stead. Her campaign slogan? - was "two Governors for the price of one!"

Now, there was a driving issue in Texas at the time that will sound somewhat familiar even today, about whether or not children were to be punished if they spoke Spanish in the public schools. They asked Ma what she thought about it, and Ma said "if the English language was good enough for Jesus Christ, it is good enough for the school children of Texas."
As Ann tells a joke, she scans the audience horizon, as if checking that no heifer has slipped out of the herd.

And you probably also don't know that the father of our country was born in Texas. And when he was just a slip of a boy, he took his little hatchet, went out into the back yard, and chopped down the family

AVE BONAR

Holland Taylor as Ann Richards: "I bet some o' you just remember ME 'cause of my *hair*."

mesquite tree. And when his father walked out into the
yard and saw the only shade for fifty miles lying dead
on the ground, he called him out and he said, "George.
Did you cut down this mesquite tree?" And George said,
"Well, yes... I cannot tell a lie, I took my little
hatchet and I cut the tree down." And his father says,
"Well, Son, we're gonna have to move to Virginia." And
George said, "Oh, Father, do we have to move 'cause I
so shamed the family by cutting down the tree?" And his
father says, "No, Son- it's because if you can't tell
a lie, you'll never amount to anything in Texas." *(She
shoots her cuffs conceitedly)*

President and members of the Board of Trustees,
esteemed faculty, proud graduates- and relieved
parents- It isn't just you pink cheeked youngsters who
face the unknown today... Our nation is in the throes
of a "commencement", if you will, more dramatic than
I have seen in my lifetime. We now move forward from
our Industrial Age into the new Information Age -- and
this enormous shift puts the burden on your generation.
Earlier in the century, the simple move from the
Agrarian Age into our industrial economy -- from the
farm to the factory floor -- asked nothing new of
America's workforce. You understand? Work still meant
having a strong back and putting in the hours to do
well. But this no longer holds true. For the computer
consoles which now run the world... a strong back, and
sweat of the brow, are not what is required. We face a
daunting change. So, look, we're all nervously twirling
our mortarboard tassels this day.

Oh, my goodness, it got so quiet in here! Come on,
y'all know every commencement speech has a gloom and
doom part. That was it.

Now, what I must do is congratulate your girls'

basketball team on landing in the top three of the
Southwestern Conference! I loved basketball when I was
at Baylor, and I am a big Lady Longhorns fan!

--When I first started going to their games, I was so
staggered to see Barbara Jordan there... Here was I,
this awe struck li'l house wife, and there was this
great American patriot, her chair pulled up to the
scorekeeper's table, and on a bad night for the team,
she'd pound that table with the flat of her hand, and
say in the voice of God, "Can we not shoot any better
than this?" Oh, man-- There was simply something about
Barbara Jordan that made you proud to be part of the
country that produced her. I still get a catch in my
throat to think that fifteen years later, she would
chair my campaign for Governor.

Well, y'all, I love being in this part of Texas! My
Daddy was born just up the road from here-- 'n' when
I was growing up in the early nineteen thirties? It
had to be unusual that a father, a simple man, didn't
go past eighth grade, would tell his little girl, his
only child, that she could do anything she wanted to
in life. But he said it a lot-- and he told me I was
really smart so often, that I believed him. Wadn't till
I got to college, th't I wondered if he might be wrong.

I suppose I owe my natural confidence to my Daddy. But
y'all-- confidence for what? When I was young- back in
the ice age- little girls did not envision careers.
Even nursing and teaching, so desperately important-
they weren't thought of as careers back then. Truth is,
they were basically j's extensions of what was expected
of women anyway.

Man, had I had a crystal ball- back there when I was
a kid in Lakeview, that wide spot in the road where I

grew up near Waco- where there was no lake to view- and had I seen that I would become Governor of the great State of Texas, the ninth largest economy in the world, I would have fallen backwards off the porch laughing!

And now, o' course, I'm this big ol' know-it-all former governor-- and I don't know if this class has any idea what happens when they invite someone who could also be their grandmother to come speak, because I have a lot of opinions. Can you imagine if I were your mother-in-law? I could fix you. But listen to me now-- there is no one here-- whose start in life coulda been more inconsequential than mine!

I tell you a little of my beginnings, because, often when I come to speak, I am greeted with this admiration that's certainly flattering... but really now, as young people you need to understand... that while I would love to be able to tell you I was fated for greatness, and groomed to lead, and blessed with genius-- as Richard Nixon said, so many years ago, "that would be wrong."

I want you to know about me that there is nothing --nothing, absolutely NOTHING- in my background, my upbringing, my native abilities, in my schooling, in my dreams, *(laughing now)* in my parents dreams for me, that would suggest to me, or anyone else -- what was to come, what I would risk, and what opportunities would fall in my lap.

You --all of you, not just the kids... you have no idea what may be in store for you, or of what you might be capable. Some of you will have dreams and plans all laid out, and by God, you gonna do it all! --Others of you have moonlight in your eyes, and no clue! You will only see your path --when you look back.

Barbara Jordan served as chair of Ann's campaign for
governor. Here the two are shown at a rally at the
electrical workers union in Houston.

I-- was in the "no clue" camp.

My childhood was as simple as a crayon drawing. My Mama, who was called Ona, was one tough bird. My Daddy, Cecil, was pure sunlight-- 'n' I see both of them in me like a swirl dip cone. I was Daddy's pride and joy, but my Mama looked at me with a narrowed eye, and pulled me through a knothole my entire childhood.

I suppose we were poor --this was the middle of the depression --but I don't like the word, I prefer "hard working." My Daddy worked for the same pharmaceutical company all his life- first as a driver, then a salesman-- and he left the house early and he came home late.

And I don't believe I ever once saw my mother idle:

We lived in a little clapboard house she basically raised up herself, drew it out with a builder, bought the materials, hired laborers in town. Mama was as hard as the nails that held that house together.

The day I was born in that house -you see, there was no star in the east - on that day, a neighbor came by to help make dinner for Mama and Daddy. But the woman didn't know a chicken needed killing, and she just couldn't do it- so my Mama, right there in the birthing bed, hunched herself up on an elbow and wrung that chicken's neck for her.

Mama said!- when she taught me to sew- that if the seam was not straight, or if the stripes didn't match on the seam, that I would have to pull every one of those stitches out with my teeth on Judgment Day!

One day I began to understand that I would never, ever,

ever please my Mother, and that's when it sorta got
funny! When I gave that keynote in Atlanta, the T.V.
Station in Waco, KWTX, set up this big ol' watch party,
and a whole lot of folks and my parents saw it on a
live feed. After the speech, I was kinda dazed, but I
knew it had been a big deal, so I call 'em up on the
telephone. And Mama says, "Ann -- Ann!... you'll never
guess what happened-- something really wonderful!"-
and I get all warm, and I say, "What, Mama, what?"
And she says, "Oh, Ann! I got to meet the Channel Ten
weatherman! *(Coming out of laughter)* Oh, God...

I tell these stories on my Mama... but I do owe her
gratitude. I got her grit. She taught me that you move
on. You don't cry over spilt milk. In fact, if my
Mama's your Mama, you better not cry at all.

Now, my father was a darling man. He usta take me
by the hand- 'n' I was this little bitty thing, and
he's six foot four... and he'd say "Let's go, Puss!"-
and he'd take me fishing, which I thought then and still
do was the grandest thing you could do. And we'd visit
the drugstore- you know- with the chairs out front...
and the barbershop, those places ol' guys gather and
sit, and joyfully greet each other- as if they hadn't
just spent the day before sitting together!

My Daddy was the greatest storyteller. Awful, bawdy
stories-just the worst! It's why I developed such a
taste for dirty jokes. I can't resist 'em, I admit it.
I wish I could tell y'all a story of his, but I can't!
They're really too nasty.

Oh, wait, now, there is one I might could tell. *(She
cocks an eye to the audience)* And I know the Board of
Trustees would be disappointed if I didn't tell one
just a little risky.

So it seems there's these three dogs are put in a pen
out at the vet's. Some little terrier type, and a
Bulldog, and a Great Dane...
and they fall to talking, wondering what they're doing
there-- and the li'l terrier says, "Oh, I got in big
trouble, I bit this little girl's ankle real bad and,
well...

I'm afraid they're gonna put me down today." And the
Bulldog says, "Why, that's terrible"-- and the terrier
asks him, "What's your story?" And the Bulldog says,
"Well, it's sorta similar... I chased our neighbor's
cat, and I caught it- and I just ripped its throat
out, and they're gonna put me down too." And they both
look over to the Great Dane, and say, "Hey, Pal, wh-
what're you in here for?" ... The Great Dane stretches
out, and says, "Well, guys, it's kinda like you. I was
just sitting in the living room the other day, and my
mistress come in out of the shower, a towel wrapped
around her, and she bent over to pick up a newspaper...
and I don't know what came over me, but I jumped up and
I mounted her." And the other two dogs go, "Oh, my God!
What are they gonna do to you?! ...'n' the Great Dane
says, "Well-- they're gonna trim my nails and try to do
something about my breath."

Like I said, a darling man. So while I wasn't groomed
for greatness, I am sure my political career rested
on the ease I felt out in the world with Daddy-- and
certainly amongst all those good old boys. Of which he
was one.

But for all that fatherly warmth-- there was something
else, too, gave me a sense of belonging in the world,
from when I was a child. Something that happened.

We were in the middle of the war... The big war, of

AVE BONAR

Ann loved the plain folk, who were as comfortable with
her as they were with themselves. She met these folks
in the Liberty County Courthouse.

course-- Japan had just entered the fray, and my Daddy was drafted into the Navy. Soon he got stationed in San Diego and had to leave us. Now, we were not a touchy huggy kinda family, but the day he left, he reached down for me and burst out crying.

After he'd been in California a few months, Mama and I just couldn't stand it. She yanked me out of school, killed every chicken we had, canned 'em, canned everything in the garden-- wedged our belongings and us in the old worn out Chrysler we had, and lit out for California. She'd never been much further than the grocery, but she drove us across the whole darn country herself. When we finally arrived, Daddy said we looked like the Grapes of Wrath.

So there I was- from this teeny, tiny crossroads in the middle of Texas- over to sprawling San Diego, where you got to look down on an ocean! I took a city bus to a big public school, with thousands of kids -- and they were all nationalities, all colors, all stripes and sizes... there were brown kids, and Italians, Asian, and Greek children, Hispanics and black students --and those kids were all exactly like me.

Oh, it was a moment to make you blink.

From then on, I just flat never understood racial prejudice. I may have only been a child, but I think I saw plain, there was a way people could live that you all would call fair play- but at the same time- I saw it was no sure thing in this world.

For where I grew up, why... segregation was... rooted!- just an unnoted aspect of every day life. So there, in my eleventh year, what with this fabulous vision of the confetti of kids who were all my new friends, my eyes

AVE BONAR

Ann attended a luncheon near Texarkana. On the drive
back to town, we crossed a bridge and saw these two
women fishing. They were mother and daughter, Virgie and
Magnolia.

popped open-- and I never knew they were shut!

Life was never the same for me. Stepped down offa that bus- and into the world.

But the passion I suddenly felt for -simple fairness- was personal. And, yeah, it became political-- but that didn't mean I'd be in politics. Shoot. It never entered my head I'd ever serve. How ridiculous! First of all... that wasn't even an option. You understand? In the fifties, women "outside the home," were sorta invisible- and unused-- which is more the point. When I was this young Austin housewife, volunteering in politics, which I did, meant I was one of the girls stuffing envelopes, and going for coffee. Period.

Now, with my young husband, David Richards, it was another story. He was a civil rights lawyer, and he knew absolutely everything. 'N' for David and me, politics was like going dancing or bowling for other couples. Hell, we were tacking posters to telephone poles on our honeymoon!

When I was a girl, back in high school, big star on the debate team and all- it made perfect sense I would fall madly in love with David Richards, and he with me. He was tall. Almost as tall as Daddy. He was really, really smart, and we loved to talk. Unlike other teenagers, he had no cruelty in him.

As a boy, he read the story of Robin Hood over and over, and he would always cry salty tears when Robin dies at the end. David wanted to protect people who needed help, too, and in a very real sense, that is what he would do with the law. Our song was Tony Bennett singing "Blue Velvet." We married at nineteen. In those days, that was not thought to be too young.

I was happy as could be. We both were. And I felt
taking care of my children and my husband was my
profession, ya know? -- all the way into the sunset...
So I set about making kids-- we quit at four- and David
made a big hit, arguing out under the trees with all
the crusty old democrats at Scholz's Beer Garden-- And
I was content just to soak it all up, knock back those
cold beers, and worship at David's shrine.

And I thought my duty in life was to be perfect.
Perfect wife, mother, lover, nursemaid, cook, you name
it! If it was in the glossy magazines, I was doing it.
I wanted to be, and I was, everything to everybody.
And if I had a spare fifteen minutes, I'd plan a big ol'
dinner party for sixty! I took the Waco Women's Club
motto as my own -- "If we rest, we rust!"-- And I did
all of it with this prideful energy that was floating
just on top of desperation. But of course, I didn't see
it that way. Not when there was a Vodka martini with a
twist waiting! And, believe me, there always was.

A-a-anyway, by then, I was already focused on the hard
practical reality of fixing stuff in my community. I
was like the poster child for Functioning Alcoholics
Everywhere. And I functioned all over the place!

And on the political front?-- W-e-e-ll --I had long
since quit getting coffee for the guy with the clipboard
and I had learned how to put together a smart campaign.
I helped several women run for office- much younger
than I, of course, women of real stature. Like Sarah
Weddington, who at a mere twenty-six had just argued
Roe v. Wade. We ran a good race, Sarah won a seat in
the Texas House, I had an adrenalin rush that should've
been illegal, and then, ya see, my job was done...
Sarah had to go to work, but I could go on home, plant

the new garden, give the dogs a tick bath --- and face once again how far apart my husband and I had grown.

I am bemused! -- that in that race track world of politics I loved, with its glamorous images of running and taking the lead and winning the roses ... I always saw myself in the stands -- I never saw myself as the horse! And nobody else threw a saddle on me either! Maybe 'cause I was like the class clown in our gang. It's very tricky when a woman is funny.

'N drinking? ~ drinking was no help, y'all. I know I crossed the line one time going to a costume party dressed as a tampon. Well -- you can sorta see it, can't ya? So, I wasn't on anybody's lips as a likely public servant.

However, I was on a fervent mission to get other women --not me, other women, and minorities, to participate in government-with this group that traveled all over the state. A very smart girl named Jane Hickie, who ran the local chapter of this group, spied me as someone who could sell this stuff like hot cakes-- so we put our act together and took it on the road, looking for women with a glint in their eye.

One fine day!-- It's always on a fine day, idn't it?-- One fine day a bunch of our politico friends came over to persuade my husband to run for county commissioner-- sort of like a "governor," on a small, local scale; it-it's executive in nature. But David was deep in civil rights lawsuits... And he says nah, he didn't want to run.

So then everyone's in our big kitchen, sitting around moping, 'n' one of them says, "Well, Ann-- why don't you run?" I think I was at the sink. There was this pause... And somebody else goes, "Hummm..." Like, did they want tomato soup or chicken noodle? I was just a fill in. Women never did those big jobs! --But see, they didn't have anyone else they could run. So- we do the precinct research, and fuss about it for weeks, and- turns out, all our pals think I got a shot!

Then, finally, my husband says, "Ann, if you don't take a chance, you'll wonder about this the rest of your life."

Well, my blood ran col'. He and I may have seemed like a permanent institution to all our friends, after- ya know- twenty-odd years, but a lot of love had gone under that bridge, and now we were pretty ragged. Somewhere I knew if I won that County Commissioner job, I could only do it whole hog. All in. I feared our marriage would not hold. And, of course, I was right! In those next first years of my public service, when my whole life was expanding -- everything that made me feel like me, was collapsing! I wasn't drinking for *nothing.*

Now, look y'all-- about the drinking-- I was fun! We had parties for absolutely no reason. And I really threw a bash if it was Thursday. I musta drunk eleven hundred thousand martinis by the time I landed in AA-- and by then, I was this big ol' county commissioner!-- So, I like to think I broke a barrier for politicians with an addiction in their past. And nowadays, Hell, you can't hardly even get into a primary unless you've done time in rehab.

I went to rehab-- 'cause a bunch of friends and family snuck up on me with this intervention deal... and I was like traumatized-- seeing all of 'em sitting there, looking like The Lord's Last Supper! I thought something had happened to one of my children! When I

got the drift-- I thought, "Well, if this isn't a pile!
You all were right there drinking with me!"

But, one by one, they all told me what I was like when
I drank-- and you... you just can't even hear that
stuff. Then one of our dearest old friends says, "Ann,
we named our only daughter after you. We want her to be
proud of you." I was on a plane to a treatment hospital
that very night. "Drunk school" we called it!

And yeah, I must've learned something about myself the
month I spent there, 'cause I was sure glad to be sober
when, pretty soon after, David and I made our good
byes. I was by then well into my forties... I had never
been alone one minute in my life. I thought if I was
not married to David Richards right into the sunset, I
was gonna die.

And when he was finally, really gone-- I am mortified
to tell you- I actually took up knitting. But time
passed... and I was still alive! And you know what? It
just seemed like a better idea to become governor of
Texas instead!

But back in that hot kitchen!- back at that cross
roads-- when he said, "you should do it, Ann" - I
froze.
And then, the clock went tick-- and I moved ahead.
And without even knowing it- I placed my bets on me.

And work, work was the best antidote for fear-- So,
I hit the gas! Besides, the notion of running was
catching on. Gears were turning, 'n' clip boards were
flying, and before I knew it, all my network of women
arrived, on their brooms, with their law degrees and
checkbooks and rolodexes. I had the sense to snag that
Jane Hickie person as campaign manager, and she may

have been fifteen years my junior but, really, she was
like a mentor to me-- and she is so wicked smart, you
don't know what the Hell she just said, but you know
it's good!

We started planning. All of us around our big ol'
dinner table! Shoot - we knew how to do it! I was
suiting up. Gosh-- I was happy... and now, there was a
glint in my eye.

Now, don't get me wrong, being a mother meant
everything to me- But my kids were pretty grown, and
here I had a chance to put to the fire things I had
stood for all my life. If I was ambitious, it's because
I know that life is not fair. I had learned that at
eleven! Life is not fair. But government should be.
(Quiet) And thus began -- my career.

I was good as a candidate over all those years only
because I connected with people. One on one, one on
one. And I also knew how to help people feel good about
themselves, that someone was payin' some attention to
them! I cared passionately about that. And it is some
hard work on the road.

Man, county commissioner for six years, then elected
up to State Treasurer for a couple of terms...Endless
campaigning! Buses, beat up ol' vans, state fairs-- Ya
ever been to a state fair? Without a hat? --Up to our
eyeballs in balloons and bar-B-que-- forging on from
town, to dusty town. You understand? Texas is bigger
than France! But fifteen years on that fast track of
Texas politics seemed to agree with me. Hey- other than
mud in your face, it's fun!

And then, outta the blue, along comes that big keynote
speech in Atlanta, and suddenly, half the damn country

--sees me as the horse. I musta been on the front page
of every newspaper in the English speaking worl'! My
supporters dropped their popcorn and burst into flame!
They turned their eyes to the governor's mansion. Ye
Gods! Did we dare? Yeah, we did.

But, lissen y'all, on paper? A woman, a divorced
woman?--
a ten-year-sober alcoholic-- and a democrat, no less!?
--running for Governor of macho, conservative Texas
-- Well, get back! That is insane! Even though I had
done really well in public service-- off the charts, if
you must know. We raised more non tax money for Texas
than all the treasurers in the history of the state
combined-- even so-- no-one thought we could really
take the Capital. But a lot of powerful people, and
everyday folk too, they just felt in their blood that--
somehow, I could. And they went with their blood.

Now y'all have to know, Texas politics is a contact
sport. No autopsy-- no foul. That campaign was the most
stressful thing I'd ever done in my life, other than
teach junior high school. But even the most brutal
gubernatorial race in recorded history couldn't knock
the wind out of our hope to make a new Texas-- *(Gentle)*
where the doors of government were OPEN, and everyone
got to come in.

The national press was all over that race. One guy
wrote, "Ann Richards has walked through fire. And the
fire lost!" And people who figured they could easily deal
with this white headed old lady, soon discovered, that
while I may have what Molly Ivins called Republican
hair- the reality is, kids, it's best you know -- I
come from Georgia prison stock!

Ann and Democratic opponent Attorney General Jim Mattox had a brief conversation at a labor convention in Austin. Former Governor, Mark White, was the third candidate in the primary race.

During the above... The phone rings. Seen in growing light, a large desk magically enters, with a huge console phone-- a credenza bearing pictures, colored files, crystal objects. A leather backed rolling desk chair. Eighteen foot high wood shuttered windows. An immense simple brass chandelier. A door leading off, flanked by splendid flags-- of the United States and of Texas. Daylight shines through the shutters.

ANN

Fifteen years after knocking on my first door, I found myself the Governor of Texas. Older and wiser, I had learned by then what not everyone knows-- it takes one person to run, and it takes quite another to actually govern.... *(There is an intercom buzzer)*

Yeah?

(Buzzer)

Nancy?

(Buzzer)

Who IS it? I'm not taking calls unless it's the president of the United States of America.

November 6, 1990, the night Ann won the governor's
race, someone handed her this t-shirt.

NANCY (V.O.)

Well, according to Bill, he still is the president, amazingly enough.

ANN

Omigod. *(Picks up receiver and hits button on 35 line phone)*
Hi ya, Kid, how are ya? Well, I tell ya, it sure does make a girl feel good a President returns her call so quick.

> *She sits at her desk or wanders, her hands are rarely still. She is a fiddler with things.*

...Yeah, it's a program we are all fired up about in Texas--
the report'll be on your desk tomorrow-- a really creative approach to ending the welfare cycle, that I genuinely, Bill, I genuinely think could be the model for the nation, and I urge you to give it your attention.
...No, yeah, the pilot program is up, it's running like gang busters in San Antonio-- Why should Washington reinvent the wheel, when Texas already has it rolling?
...Thank you, Mr. President.
...Oh, I think Senator Kerry's doin' great!.. I'll keep October clear as I can-- you need me in Massachusetts, I'm all in-- 'money, marbles and chalk'
...I love you too, Bill. Bah. *(She hangs up)*

ANN

Nancy, this Edward person, the Ivy League guy handling

the Mexico State visit-- Did he call? Or just send this
stupid fax?

                    Nancy (V.O.)
No. He hasn't called.

                    ANN

Chicken shit.

                    NANCY (V.O.)

And Governor, I have not found one of your children...
I left messages for Clark and Ellen and Dan, but
Cecile's machine didn't even pick-up.

                    ANN

Keep trying all of 'em!
This trip's in ten days-- no hotels, no liaison to
President Salinas!-- So much for diplomatic relations.
How dare this guy..?
Nancy, did the Chief of Staff make it back from
Washington yet?

                    NANCY (V.O.)
Yeah, I think she just did.

                    ANN

(*She punches speed dial*) Oh, my Lord, no airplanes--
(*On phone*) Hi, welcome home. Mary Beth, that ass-hole
Edward, doing Mexico -- that guy couldn't organize a
circle jerk.
...I don't care who hired him-- won't be the first time
Cathy Bonner was blinded by a cute butt.
...Just roll him back to Commerce like the spare tire

he is. And it's a State visit, for God's sake-- find
somebody sharp to take over who's at least from Mexico!

Now, Mary Beth, I know I said I wouldn't ask you to
work at night, if I could possibly avoid it, and I
haven't, you know? I mean -- look, I'm not asking you
to come to this meeting tonight, when you're just back
and all-- but tomorrow is that big reception for all
the governors, and I need you to stay and walk me into
the room. Just get me started.
...Hell, no, I'm not gonna' ask him! Why do I always
get drug around by the Lieutenant Governor? Bob Bullock
and I aren't even speaking this week! Why can't you do
it? I am so weary of fussing with this man- Why can't
my chief of staff bring me in?
...Oh, c'mon, you'll be home early, darlin'. Just get
me through the door. I'm fine once I'm in the swing.

...Oh, this thing tonight is just-- I need some help
about this kid's scheduled to die. I seem to be
considering a stay.
...No one around here remembers a Governor giving one,
so it musta been a long time ago! (She stands in the
shuttered afternoon light, looking down) Mary Beth, go
over to your windows and look down at the front steps.
Do you have a crowd gathering over there yet?
...Yeah, well, it's all over the news now the Pope is
horning in on this, for Godssakes. The Lord's eye may
be on the sparrow, but the Pope is lookin' at Texas.
...No, that case comes up next month- this is the one
where that abused kid raped and killed the seventy six
year old nun.
...I know, who can bear it? My Mama is seventy six.
...I'm sure a stay will bring ashes down on our head,
but--
... Oh, yeah, I agree, no, I have to go with what I
feel--

But listen, I gotta run, I can't even face that music
'til tonight, after El Paso. ...O.K. Bye--

...What?? Oh, for pity's sake, I was not mean to
Suzanne, I beat on her because if I don't, she will
NEVER finish writing a speech! Hell, I am the one under
a magnifying glass around here, I always have to be on
-- if I can't let my hair down with the people I love,
when can I?
...Oh, very funny, Mary Beth. Very funny. Look -- I, I
do "let go and Let God"...but HE can't make Suzanne do
anything, either.
...OK, bye. *(Hanging up and yelling)*

Nancy, get me my travel aide. I think it's Donisi
today.

                        NANCY (V.O.)

He just stepped out, he's been trying to get something
to eat...

                        ANN

Well, I need him... *(She hits speed dial)*

                        NANCY (V.O.)
(Under her breath) Oh, boy. I'll send someone to catch
him...

                        ANN

(On phone) Ellen, there you are! Your mother here-- I
haven't heard from any of you kids about our long week-
end- I'm just sitting here assuming you're all coming?
...Well, Ok, then! Listen, I want you to go rent a

small van, charge it to me, and bring that set of red
chairs in Cecile's attic down to the beach-- I want 'em
for the housekeeper's daughter.
...Darlin', you do this for me and you ain't ever gohn'
have to cook or wash up, you'll be "the princess of the
van".
...Now, you telephone everyone to hit the King's Inn
around lunch time and then I'll take off forty-five
minutes after you do, my guys drive me a hundred miles
an hour.
...No, you make the calls, Cecile is just nuts with
those twins.

So, Dan tells me Clark's still making noises about not
coming down this year. Did you talk to him?
...Well, it is just ludicrous, this thing over
charades, good God. Put him on the same team as Jane--
she's the one made him so mad. *(Buzzer)*
Darlin', I gotta get on the stick. King's Inn. Fried
Shrimp!!!
...OK, Bye. *(To intercom)* Yeah?

                    NANCY (V.O.)

I've been holding Donisi on the line. He's wasting
away --

                    ANN

Nancy, this whole damn pile of stuff in the orange
folder can't be essential..? I will be signing till the
crack of Doom...

                    NANCY (V.O.)

Yes, Governor, I was careful to put in only what has to
go out tonight.

Holland Taylor as Ann Richards: Making up on
the run.

ANN

God. *(She hits a lighted button)* Donisi, ya know- we
have this whole big award thing tonight, I have to go
back over to the mansion and tart myself up. So meet me
over there in an hour.
Now, I'm 'bout outta my mind today-- do not let me
leave for the airport without my blue tote, and you
keep it with you. It's the death penalty file. I hafta
fly right back and meet with General Counsel on it
tonight. Damn, this will be the latest I ever called in
a decision. So we're gonna split before the dinner--
and don't let anybody engage me, just shovel me out and
back to the Mansion by 8:30.
...And j's keep your nose in a book, Mr. Chatterbox
--first chance I'll have to think all day'll be on the
plane.
What else? --Oh, yeah. I can't be out of reach if the
Court has some action on this case, so bring the air
phone. Bring the back-up, too-- and whyn't you charge
'em this time, just for laughs.
...OK. See ya over there... *(Hangs up)*

Nancy? Do we still have shoe sizes for everybody in the
outer office? From when we gave the sneakers?

NANCY (V.O.)

I've got a list tucked away.

ANN

Make me a copy.
I don't suppose by any miracle Suzanne has faxed my
speech...

NANCY (V.O.)

She says she's going to FAX it right to the El Paso
Hotel.

ANN

O-o-o-h, she's gonna FAX it over there?? OH, w-e-ell,
that jus' fills me with confidence. Goddammit, I can't
wing that speech! And I'm s'posta talk about every one
of those awardees!! What is it with Suzanne?! If she
wasn't so darn good I would just --pinch her head off.
(Turning back to Nancy)

Oh, so -call over to the boot factory, you know, that
girlfriend o' mine's store in El Paso, they're having
a big sale-- And somebody make fresh coffee, this stuff
will kill us all--*(Signing papers)* They'll find thirty
people lying dead on the floor, it's gonna look like
Jonestown around here. --Where in God's name are my
kids??? *(Buzzer)*

NANCY (V.O.)

I got your Boot lady.

ANN

(Picking up phone, calling back) And Nancy, get me that
son of a bitch on the Insurance Board-- He thinks he's
gonna play me! Wait'll I blow some smoke up his ass.
(Into phone) Hey, d'you hear all that? It's Ann!
...Listen, Darlin', I'm flying to a thing out your way
tonight, and we'll drive right past your place, so I
thought I could hit the sale and buy a big bunch of
boots for my secretarial staff here.

...Probably eight or nine pair.

...No, I wanna pick 'em out-- We'll just throw 'em in the trunk and fly 'em home.

...Oh, sure-- I'm happy to say 'hi' to everyone, but warn 'em we're going through like a dose of salts, we can't linger.

...Thanks a million. See ya then!

                    NANCY (V.O.)

I've got Jaston Williams again, Ann. Susan Rieff says he's not going to back off. She got nowhere with him.

                    ANN

Well, shit, Nancy.

                    NANCY (V.O.)

He's been trying to catch you all morning -- yesterday, too.

                    ANN

(She pounds the desk) Susan Reif is supposed to be my junk yard dog! I have to pick my battles! I cannot airlift that nuclear dump away from his mama's town-- that is federal stuff, not state!! Goddammit. (Resigned) Well, tell him I love him, make time for him to come in. What am I gonna do with him? Ye Gods, I don't have to worry about my enemies, my friends are gonna kill me! (Turns to signing. Stops. Thinks)

(Punching intercom on phone) Oh, for Pete's sake, Ann, why do you keep on fighting this?

NANCY (V.O.)

Go ahead, Governor.

ANN

(Thinking, crosses to Nancy's door) Yeah-- Nancy,
tomorrow I wanna see that brief on nuclear waste out in
Hudspeth county. But also- I wanna see those provisions
in our border treaty that protect the Rio Grande River.
She lifts a corner of the flag.
How in the world did this dumb fringe come loose
off this flag here?? Are you moonlighting as a Drum
Majorette?? *(Returns to desk)*

Oh, Rats, I forgot. Goddamn, I can't believe I am so
stupid. Listen, I have a task for, uh, uh-- oh, that
little round girl I like in Appointments-- Sandra! She
was so sharp doin' that interview the other day-- You
know what, pick some cute trinket outta my "good job"
drawer and put it on her desk when you leave tonight.

Now, all those scraps of paper and cards from those
folks I met at the Brownsville demonstration-- put 'em
on a list so I can send notes. I never saw such a bunch
of hard working people... how good is Sandra's Spanish?

NANCY (V.O.)

Serviceable. I mean, Sandra's born here, Ann, in
Seguin.

ANN

Oh. Well, she better brush up, 'cause now she's their
point person. Tell her this one woman in particular,
her name is on the back of that colored Saints' prayer

card you got there,-- Sandra is to track her down
today. The woman brought her son with her. Probably
nine years old. This child lives in a house with no
water, and no electricity, and I don't know how-- but
he is gonna be something.

We're putting an arm around this boy's shoulder. I
want him up here... OK, where is my blue binder?? *(She
looks around, stands up to snatch the calendar from the
credenza)* I want him up here for children's day at the
mansion, next week-- with all those fat capital brats--

Nancy, I'm looking at my calendar-- Why in Hell is
there nothing but one thousand erasures on the FOURTH?!
Goddammit, call down to scheduling, they're supposed
to keep this binder up to date! *(Throwing her voice to
the outer office)* Does anyone around here do their job?
(Silence. Back to signing)
-- And try Suzanne again. I'm this close to sending
somebody over there. She's probably got a chair up
against the door by now.

                    NANCY (V.O.)
OK, Governor, I have Sally for you, from scheduling...
(Quick) Now, she's new, Ann, so don't make her—

                         ANN

(Into phone) This is Ann Richards. Are you the girl
with the green eyes and the bangs?
...I want to suggest to you that you rethink the bangs.
You don't want to look like a little girl in an office
situation, it's hard enough for women to be taken
seriously as it is!
Now, I'm here looking at my schedule, and why in the
world is the fourth of July empty?
...Well, my Gaaahhhd, if that was cancelled, why wasn't

I informed? There's an idea for you. And why wasn't
something filled in from the wait list?
...Oh! (Speechless for a moment) Uh, uh... I see. Well,
I suppose it's darling that you all want to give me a
"day off," (wipes her eyes) Oh, my God.

What is your name again?
...Sally. Well, Sally, you are new here, so let me
bring you up to speed. I did not get myself elected
Governor of the great State of Texas, to spend this
Nation's most important holiday loafin' with my family
and sitting on my ass-- pick some little town, -and find
me a parade, Sally! (She hangs up, peeks over at Nancy
for a giggle, and goes back to signing)

Nancy, what did I do when I got in from Johnson City
this morning?

                    NANCY (V.O.)

You went right into the staff meeting. Then you had the
shake 'n' bake with the guys from Northrop Grumman, cut
the ribbon on our day care rooms-- then the Catholic
Bishops' emissary came, then--

                    ANN

...Then I ate lunch at my desk --and I've been here
chained to this telephone ever since. I don't believe
I've been to the bathroom.

                    NANCY (V.O.)

Well... you would know, Governor.

ANN

(Rummages under desk for shoes) Oh, I hardly pay any attention.

Well, I'm gonna go now. Back in ten minutes sharp! *(Grabs purse as she strides off)* And if my Mama calls, don't tell her where I went. *(Light, to Nancy as she crosses proscenium)* She says it's a sign of weakness. *(Laughs)*

INTERMISSION

ACT TWO

*We hear the hum of the office
and Ann using her "outside"
voice.*

                    ANN (O.S.)

Well, I-I-I-I am a new woman! *(Blowing in)* Man, there is
nothing like being swarmed by thirty little girls from
Brownie Troop Five twenty-six in a four-stall ladies'
room to put things in perspective!

                    NANCY (V.O.)

Governor, the President needs you to get back. What do
you want me to do?

                    ANN

Well, go ahead and call him. Oh, hey. Look up that
documentary guy, Tommy somethin', who did the Roe v. Wade
story. Wadn't I supposed to phone him in a quote after
the pro-choice march? Weren't you supposed to remind me?
If I missed his deadline, I'm going to blame you.

                    NANCY (V.O.)

I'll find him. It's a Boston station. Governor, This is
the president.

                    ANN

(On phone) You just can't get enough of me, can ya?
...Yes, I am as strong as mustard gas. What's up?
...Um-hmm. Well, I'd put cash money on a barrel to see
Barbara Jordan keep her cool around Clarence Thomas.

But I don't know that she could go on the Supreme
Court. Well, her health is so -- bad. And what with the
wheel chair and all?
...Oh, no, Bill, she's always in it now. Still does her
ethics seminars for me, though. Lemme send Jane out to
Onion Creek to talk with her. Jane's only one I got
smart enough to go.
...Yes, it is a grand notion! I will get back to you.
Thank you, Mr. President. *(She hangs up)*
I think Barbara might have too much sense to go on the
Supreme Court.
Nancy, find Jane and ask her to telephone me tonight
around uh, uh, eleven. Tell her to hold onto her hat.

NANCY (V.O.)

All right. *(Then)* The reporter's on. And the deadline
is today.

ANN

To-DAY! *(Body English)* Sometimes I can't even believe
how sharp I am. *(Picking up phone)* Hi, Tommy!
...Well, I remember men who care about Choice.
...I do. You wanna tape like a forty-five second quote,
right?
...OK, hit "record."
...Oh, Honey, this is a subject on which I am always
loaded for bear.
...Ya ready? Here we go. *(Public voice)* I think it is
really important, not only that we talk about a woman's
right to choose, but what about this current attitude
towards children who are already on this earth? They
say "there's no money to help the children you already
have, but, tsk, tsk, we're gonna force you to have some
more you can't afford..."
And listen here, Americans want to take care of their

parents and grandparents, but these right-wingers tell
us, "if you can't pay for doctors or nursing homes,
that is tough-- You take your elderly parents back in!"
And we say "but...   but, wait a minute, this is 1993
-- everybody in our home works. There isn't anybody
home to take care of our parents! -- and the government
should live up to the promise their social security
taxes paid for." How's that, Tommy, d'you get what you
need?
...Well, Young Man, thank you-- and thank you for what
you do. *(She hangs up)*

NANCY (V.O.)

Ann, I've got your son, can you speak to him now? Dan
says he's only on a teeny break. And, then, uhm, David
Miller needs to talk with you urgently. There's a
problem-- *(Clearing her throat, speaking forcefully)*
You have to pay for one of the planes he put you on--
it can't be a gift. He doesn't want to come up here to
see you, he's too scared --but it seems he's got to
cover the expense today...

ANN

Oh, well, just shoot me now.... *(Picking up phone,
calling out to Nancy.)*
Put him through when I'm done with Dan.

(To phone) Brother, it's your Mama. Listen, I need you
to check who all wants to go fishing, I have to call
down and reserve boats. You let me know tomorrow ayem.
...Hey, you get to bring the ham this year, I'm getting
Clark to do the turkey.
...No, I'm not asking Cecile to cook meat, when she
doesn't eat it and doesn't like handling it, for
Heaven's sake -- she's gohn' make pies like she always does.

...Now, Dan, when we play charades, for God's sake, quit tormenting Clark, and give him something a person can act. We have almost lost him over this. I don't know why you are so hard on him -- I wish I had a baby brother who adored me.

...Oh, don't test my patience, Dan. Spare me the drama. I'm runnin'.

...OK, Son, Bye. *(She hears the call waiting and clicks to another line)*

ANN

David Miller, this is your Boss. You don't want to see me? What's the deal?

...You have got to be joking. Eight thousand dollars??-- I'm not gonna pay that.

Oh, get back, how could this man LEND me his planes if he has a kid in jail, is he out of his mind? And you! D-d-did you not VET this guy?? ...Well. This is just the biggest screw up of your young life, idn't it? I- I can't even believe this. My dealings have always been impeccable! Jesus, Mary, and Joseph! Goddammit!

Man-oh-man, *(She is rummaging around noisily in purse, whining)* I am not a rich woman-- This is, like-- more'n a month's pay! And I cannot go to campaign funds for this! I am not about to drag the sack to donors who're generous to me because they believe I am good for Texas, and tell 'em I need a whole big bunch o' more money 'cause this kid I stupidly gave an important job to screwed up!

... David Miller-- are you crying? Quit that. Nobody's dead. *(She is at the desk writing the check.)*

What is the amount-- eight thousand seven hundred and what?...

...Oh, yeah, no, no, don't let's forget that last two

bits. I will leave the check on my desk. I'm taking off
for El Paso. And I don't want to see you, either.
She hangs up violently.
Nancy, call over to the bank and warn 'em a big check's
coming through for eight grand and change and they
should just-- I don't know, slide it over from savings,
I guess. *(Childish complaint)* Shit. *(She sits grumpily.*
Signs letters)

NANCY (V.O.)

Ann, your mother's neighbor called to ask what to do,
seems Ona is up on the roof cleaning out the gutters
and the lady is beside herself...

ANN

(Laughing) Oh, my God... Well, I'll bet Mama thinks
the rain is gonna take out all those nineteen cent
periwinkles she just planted, so-- just say there's
nothin' to do -- but leave her to it.

NANCY (V.O.)

All right. I'll tell 'er."

ANN

(Laughing with delight over at Nancy) As if falling off
a house would hurt my Mama!
(She signs in silence. Then, with rue and a grudge)

ANN

Nancy-- Call that fool David Miller-- and get his shoe
size... and put him on the boot list, too. And if he
asks why you want it, just tell him he ain't on a "need

to know" basis around here! *(Signs more)*
Anything from Suzanne?

NANCY (V.O.)

I'm sorry, Ann. No.

ANN

Gaahhhdddammit. *(Intimately, to heaven)* When will I
learn? What is the matter with me, that I would endure
this... *(punching a speed dial)* I'm not standing for
it, I -- Suzanne!! You know I'm walking out the door in
two minutes, so once again you have left me high and
dry, and if you don't get that speech to me, I will let
all those people in El Paso down, and plus look like
a horse's ass on the news tonight, so my question for
you is this-- do you want to kill me? Just give me one
good reason, I don't need three, just one reason why I
shouldn't just hire any of those boys out of Washington
or New York who can write like crazy and who would kill
a puppy for your job. I am the fucking Governor of
Texas! "N' we worked that speech!-- All you had to do
was type it up, and I can't believe --- *(She suddenly
stops, stands stunned, and then wrestles with the phone
in a brief fit. She sits down and affects a posture of
serenity, but suddenly punches the speed dial again.
Waits. She speaks… "more in sorrow than in anger")*

...Well. To add insult to injury, your answering
machine just cut me off. Suzanne, when I think of the
opportunities to shine this job has given you- I just
marvel that you don't spring up in the morning and rush
to your desk in gratitude.
You're just sitting there, aren't you, you're drinking
a warm beer -- and you're thinking, "Oh, she'll get
over it..." Well, don't count on it, Suzanne-- that's--

all I have to say. Don't count on it. *(She hangs up)*
God, I need an AA meeting. If I had 'The Big Book' I'd
kill her with it.

Oh, my God, Nancy, look at the time... I haven't caught
all my kids! Where is that Clark?
She fetches a red sewing ball from the partners' desk
front drawer, punches a speed dial, takes receiver and
heads towards the flag, which she lifts and quickly pins
the fringe while talking.

(On the phone) Well, Hi-i-i-i-i. It's your Mother.
...Well, Clark, yeah-- I heard that, but as the kids
say-- that doesn't work for me.
...Oh, C'mon-- You have to come, you have to fish with
us! Listen, it's your turn to do the turkey this
year... No, Dan's bringing the ham.
...Well, ok, then, order one from Rovan's - but, boy,
you better call them now. Oh, you know what, never mind,
I will cook the turkey myself! ...Now-- Clar- Clar-
*(She looks heavenward, then listens to his complaint,
elbows on her knees)*

...Clark, for pity's sake, get over it! Charades is
just a game! Nobody could have done "The Rob Lowe Sex
Tapes." I don't know why you get so upset --everybody
knows you're the smartest person in the room!
...Well, get yourself on Jane's team, and you can be
mean as a snake, too!
... *(Tenderly)* Awww, Cla-r-rk. "Move on!"
...OK. Love ya, Bah.
She returns to the orange file of documents, which she
continues to sign.
Nancy, call over to General Counsel's office, and find
Talbot. Find Bill Cryer too... He will have to write a
press release big time.

                        NANCY (V.O.)

Talbot called a little bit ago saying he was just then
leaving the Attorney General's, he knows to speak with
you regarding tonight. I told him you already had the
death packet with you.

                          ANN

Well, but then where is he? What is the matter with
him? He knows we have to do this, *(Punches speed dial)*
I'm getting on an airplane! *(Returns to signing)* Why
must I ride herd on everyone?!

...Bill Cryer! Fancy finding the press secretary at his
desk! Listen, I hope you haven't got some new girl
setting her hair on fire over you-- I need you at the
Mansion at 8:30 to meet about this capital case. Right
now I'm feeling in my gut I just might stay this guy's
sentence, and if I do, our press release has to be
ready.
*(She is suddenly pissed off, strides around the desk.
Scoops off her shoes)*

Cryer, why in Hell haven't you gotten one of your hot
shot Pulitzer reporter buddies to do a big piece in the
newspaper about what governors can do or can't do with
these cases? Why aren't you on top of this? People don't
even know what a stay is-- they're callin', begging me
to give a pardon, and they have absolutely no idea that
only the board has that power! Not that the board ever
would do it. And if the public is so in the dark, I
feel like I'm pushing a rope in front of me!

...Well, you ain't making your presence felt, 'cause I
can't catch a break with the press-- Right now on the
news they're saying Governor Richards "did not take"

AVE BONAR

AVE BONAR

When Ave Bonar edited photos after a dress rehearsal, she saw the image on top and thought about the time she was with Ann in Washington, DC. Ann had bought some tennis shoes and decided to put them on, right on the street.

Mother Teresa's call! I was giving a speech!-- it's not like I hung up on her.
(_She is leaning towards the tall windows, afternoon light through the shutters. We hear the distant chanting_)

...OK, you get started writing the shortest statement we can make. And you better write it so my Mama can understand it.

(_Buzzer_)

NANCY (V.O.)

It's David Talbot.

ANN

Yeah, don't let him go anywhere. Now, Billy-- about my pitching that fit at the airport yesterday. I guess I flamed your ass. I s'pose I owe you an apology. --Well, y'ain't gettin' one. See ya over there.
(_She punches the button to switch calls_)

Talbot-- I hired you as my General counsel 'cause you are one smart lawyer, 'n' I love you to death -and there is not one black person in the state of Texas who isn't proud of you. But- I read your very long summary-- and, and, I thought you're supposed to make me understand better, not make me want to pull my hair out!
...Look, Talbot, you are the law-yer, and I am the Gov-ern-or, you have to explain the options this guy has before the law, and you have to recommend, for Heaven's sake -- and why on earth would you cite a bunch of cases as if I knew what all these precedents were... are you writing for the Harvard Law Review- or are you

helping me wade through this-- this mare's nest?
...I don't want you to be sorry, I want you to do your job.

Now, listen-- it's getting a little crazy over here.
The Amnesty people are doing a die-in on the Capital
steps -- so you better come in the side doors, and I'm
not kidding- they will know who you are. Yeah, and
I've got every Catholic bishop in the state, plus all
the nuns from that poor nun's convent, delivering me
letters today begging me to give this man a pardon.
Mother Teresa called to lean on me--
... Well- from India, I guess-- and now they've
brought me this letter from, who is this? The Papal
Nuncio, with a message from the Pope, it's got seals
and ribbons-- looks like a Christmas present. Think of
that, Talbot, the Pope has an opinion on this case. And
you don't.

...You say that every time, but if I take it as a given
someone actually ending up on death row means every
avenue of the law has already been exhausted, then wh-
wh-what is this deal? Some meaningless exercise?
...Well, that is sm-a-ll comfort. So, I need you
tonight at the Mansion about 8:30. John Hannah will be
there. And Bill Cryer, of course. I need some help.

...Well, first, the nitty-gritty is, (A huge suck of
air) I need to look at 'clemency' as a way to take
a stand. If there is no legal avenue that lets us
take into account this guy's childhood abuse -- and
if there's no law or statute, that protects him
from getting the needle, though- ya know, he's only
seventeen when he killed her-- I want to know whether
my simply taking a stand of clemency, could, given
those issues, could put some attention on what might be
viewed as inadequacies in the law?
...Well, tell me what you think-- come on, Talbot.

...Yes, I am. I'm considering a stay.
...Look! -- the guy started out in life with NO chance.
The whole deal is pitif-
(She lurches towards the chair, interrupting Talbot)

...But, --if his lawyer was so negligent, how can it be
there's no way to introduce that now?
-God, this is a quagmire. Texas can't go on this way.
(Sweeping it away. Sitting in the DL college chair)

Truth is I find I am so affected by these nuns forgiving
him. That old girl lived in that convent more than half
a damn century. Those Sisters were all she had. That's
what they wrote me. "We are her family." And they knew
this guy-- just a pasty face ne'er do well. Some dim
eyed kid who slouched around their neighborhood. --They
want me to stop this! They forgive him. --But I know
they don't understand- that I can give him thirty days,
and then there's nothing to keep him alive, not one
day, not a minute after that month goes by.

Well, I'm gohn' tell you right now, --I'm gonna do this
thing. --And more people will protest a stay than give
a damn we put him down-- like he's an animal.
...All right. 8:30. And Talbot, tomorrow, whyn't you
come over 'n' have lunch with a bunch of us at the
mansion? We'll eat at the big table with the heavy ol'
cloth, and china, 'cos we're so civilized --and we know
what we're doing, don't we? Bah. *(She drops on an elbow
and then lowers down to the desk, her head on her hand)*

NANCY (V.O.)

(Mild) Governor? Are you off?

ANN

(She hangs up?) Do we have any cookies out there?

Firstborn grandchild, Lily Adams, sometimes attended
campaign events.

NANCY (V.O.)

You ate 'em all.

ANN

I'm not taking any calls. I've got to get ready.

NANCY (V.O.)

Well, Ann-- I've got Lily waiting, she's so excited about something, I did tell her you were here-- Sorry.

ANN

(*Desperately biting off a corner of chocolate*)
Lily belle! How's my nearly perfect grand baby?
...You did! Well, I expect you to be the smartest one. Did they give you a prize?
...Ohhh, "Charlotte's Web", I love that book. Now, you're coming with me and Barbara Jordan to the Lady Longhorns game!
...Well, we can play Gin Rummy, too! But now, Lily-- listen to me. You only pick up face cards if you really need 'em, not just 'cause they're pretty, or to steal that queen I want-- You just gohn' get stuck with all those high points, you understand? You know how we add 'em all up at the end?
...Well, 'course I beat you, your Mammy is a shark. Now, I gotta go work, but I do need your Mama.
...I love you... (*Waits for Cecile to get on the line*)

-- How are you, Darling?
...Well, shoot, what do you expect, Cecile-- you have new twins, you are certifiably insane. But ain't nobody gonna' give you a blue ribbon for working yourself to death. You need some help.

...Now, Darling, can you do the pies?
...Oh, gol-LY, that's fabulous. You're my star!
...Yeah, no, Clark is coming, but he's still cranky. We just pair Clark with Jane-- it'll be fine.

...Yeah, I'm jumping on my broom, too.
...We'll see ya down there! BYE.
(Yelling off) Nancy, I'm out of here. Everything waits till tomorrow. *(She gathers her purse, and puts on lipstick)* God, I wish I had a Luanne Platter "to go."

                    NANCY (V.O.)

I have Bob Bullock screaming that you were supposed to call him today, and he needs you to get on the horn right now. He says he isn't gonna' talk to any of your hairy legg-ed zoo-girls.

                    ANN

No day would be complete without a shot from Bullock...!
She throws the Hershey's in her purse, slaps the orange folder closed, puts check under a paper weight, the office around her dims, and the light on the college chair brightens a little...
The orange folder stuff is all signed, I'm leaving a check for David Miller on my desk, under the blue armadillo... and you tell Bob Bullock he can stick a broom up my ass and I'll sweep out the office for him, but I cannot take another call!

                    NANCY (V.O. *her voice an echo*)

All right, Governor, and I will be sure to give Mr. Bullock your message... *(ANN flashes a smile over at Nancy...)*

---

*The chandelier dims out as
the chair glows in bright
light. ANN starts over to it,
remembers her shoes, nips back
for them-- she sits to put
them on.*

ANN

Can you imagine if I left these behind? I'm getting so
forgetful, soon I'm gohn' be able to hide my own Easter
eggs. *(She looks back towards the office)*

After four years of this mad intensity, came re-
election time, even though my popularity in the polls
was stronger than ever it was, I did not win my second
term. Everybody's brother-in-law had opinions as to
why, but rehashing all that crappy dirty tricks stuff
j's didn't interest me much.

I'll tell you what, though- if I got turned out over
my concealed weapons veto-- without which- every Tom,
Dick, and Harry could jus' walk into your home, or your
place of business, packing heat!!-- then I say "So be
it!"- and sayonara! More guns in people's pockets meant
more people dead. There was no compromise to be had.

Now, I did tell 'em, I tole 'em I might could consider
a law that let guys carry guns hanging from a chain
around their neck--- That way, we could say, "look out,
he's got a gun." And the idea of women carrying guns
around for protection? Give me a break, Gladys. There's
not a woman in Texas could find a gun in her purse.

All that aside- *(A smile)* Where was the sense in
looking back?

It was over.

(She emphatically lifts herself out of the chair) Well,
nobody likes gettin' beat! But I mourned that loss very
briefly, and I'm not kiddin'. If I felt a lingering
sorrow, it was for all my supporters- and my staff--ya
know? Those couple, three hundred people- who worked so
terrifically hard for me, especially the women, who also
looked to me for inspiration. Feeling that you've let
someone down is just-- the worst thing for me.

My little granddaughter Lily asked me, "Mammy, does
this mean you don't have a job?" I said, "Darlin',
it means everyone you know doesn't have a job! *(She
laughs)*

I have to confess, I wadn't gonna miss the stress.
But I did miss the children in the classrooms- those
kids who usta grab me around the knees... and I
think of the old people- who really need a voice
when they're trapped in wheelchairs in dirty nursing
homes. The person who holds this office really must
have a conscience to know- that how they direct this
government dramatically affects the lives of real
people, who are counting on them.

But in political life, truth be told, as your tenure
comes to an end, dudn't matter what side you're on, the
forces are already gathering to dismantle what you've
done, 'fore your desk chair is even cool.

The good news is, we had rung a bell they could never
unring!

... More important than legislation, more important
than vetoes, and the bully pulpit-- was our promise
that we would put together a government of citizens-

that for once, looked like the population of the state!
Where there would be no persons in all of Texas, who
didn't see others serving in office, who looked just
-like -them.

'Bout three thousand appointments to office-- many of
them female, Hispanic, Black, Gay, Asian, Disabled -
Republican! We didn't care about the flak. We did it,
and we didn't look back-- and I'll tell you what. An
awful lot of folks were extra proud of their state.

And on a personal note, let me just say-- you haven't
lived till you've been Governor of Texas.
*(She goes to the desk, picks up the bible, flips pages
quickly)*

Following an old tradition, I marked a passage in the
Good Book for the incoming Governor: Amos 5:15, "Hate
the evil, and love the good, and establish justice in
the court."

> *The entire Governor's office
> slides into darkness, Ann
> watching it go in that old
> lady, "palms up" hands on back
> of hips stance. In half-light,
> a steel and glass table, a
> modern telephone and neat
> stack of files on it, with a
> smart modern chair, appear
> downstage right.*

I loved that when the new Governor asked my comptroller
John Sharp whether he wanted to be called Mr.
Comptroller or Mr. Sharp, and how had Governor Richards
addressed him? -- John said, "She just called me
Darling."

Now, y'all... While it was the greatest honor of my life
to serve Texas as its governor, and j's wonderful to
come to know its people... it was my job. It wasn't me.

Walking out of the governor's office- I was sixty- I had
no house, no big ol' white car anymore, and no cash to
speak of. I thought, well--? Shoot. I guess I could
keep on giving talks- I enjoy that-- 'n' now I can get
paid for it! Maybe I'd have one, two- maybe three
years' "shelf life," and I could speak about the things
that mattered to me.
But what about after my shelf life "expiration date"..?
In the wee hours, I did wonder if my age old fear would
come true -- I'd end up in a trailer in my daughter
Ellen's driveway. You laugh, but you'd be surprised how
many women feel like that.

So there I was-- Out of office, on the streets, and up
in the air. But before I could open a bait & tackle
stand- which seemed like a good idea at the time- lo
and behold, half the civilized world was at my door!
I can't even tell you, the speeches I was invited to
give- the Boards I was asked to sit on-- and all the
T.V. talk shows! --You know, my friend Cathy Bonner
says I was born under a special star, and sometimes I
think that's true, 'cause listen to what happened!

Comes along these hotshot guys, who asked me to be
a consultant with them, and help big deal clients
strategize through crises. Ya know, like say- a Martha
Stewart, or an international bank-- uh, Lockheed
Martin-- stuff like that. They needed a person who, just
for starters, could get anyone in the country on the
telephone. *(Modestly)* Well- yeah. Wait! It gets better.
(Calliope music plays faintly)

So here we are-- Outta the blue, in my seventh decade,
... begins a new chapter of my life, where I was
twirled around on the most unlikely and colorful
carnival ride you could imagine... Because, good God,
can you believe this? --
Merry lights burn through the scrim, a New York Bridge
against the sky.
--They had me open an office in New York City!

So there I went!- From a tree shaded capital- from
Piney Woods, rough rivers and hills-- *(She crosses in
front of the glass desk)* -over to a world of glass and
steel, and impossible heights-- Why, why from my window
I could almost see the curvature of the earth! And all
those people--! I was terrified! I was thrilled! --And,
man, did I hear America singing.

Now, listen to me. Get this. The day- I mean the day-
I came to New York, to begin this job, was 9/11. *(The
skyscraper view appears. She leans, her arms spread
as she rests her hands on the glass)* 'N' do you know,
for all the glories of that town, it was that event
that made me proud now I was a New Yorker, too-- and
that when so many people were too scared even to visit
New York, we were setting up camp. *(She sits and looks
through a stack of papers)*

SANDRA? Sandra- Check again and see if Suzanne e-mailed that
draft. Ima hafta take a stick to her. *(Calling off)* You
know what? Just call her. Use the fax line, maybe she
won't see it's us. *(She is glancing at a laminated page
on the glass desk)*

Sandra, this itinerary here for Chicago? Google me up
stuff on whoever else is on the dais at this dinner.
Wait a minute!- You got me going direct from China to
Israel next month... I told you, I have the Human Rights

After she left the Governor's office, "Ann" pushed her podium aside to make way for her new life. Holland Taylor is shown in rehearsals before a performance.

Campaign event tucked in there- I'm not gohn' cancel on them. I told you I accepted that. *(She is looking through a few pieces of mail)*
I'm pretty sure I did. *(Off a letter)* Tell Larry King - *(She glances at desk calendar)* that - yes, I can do his show next week.

Oh, call over to that Disney Guy, and ask what Sunday I can buy five good seats for the "Lion King" matinee-- Man, this is gonna be like my seventh time at that show. *(Opening an envelope, pulling out contents)*...I could play Simba's Mama by now. *(Crosses slightly up stage)* Get another seat 'n' you come again too! Do you believe we get to do stuff like this?

Awww! Lookit this crossword puzzle Bill Clinton sent. The dog did it with a fountain pen! Let me just... *(She is hitting a speed dial)* Hunh, "Politico Richards" is the clue. My Mama would hate--
...Hey, there, Bill! Oh, yeah, I got it- and I know perfectly well you just wanted me to take note you worked it in ink.

And Clinton? I'm sorry if I was mean to you at the Party Unity Dinner, but I thought I'd die laughing-- Five former presidents and vice presidents stomping around, pumping fists, 'n' high fivin'-- all to the music from Star Wars?! Jus' trying to get you guys to sit down was like herding cats.
...Love ya, Darlin'. Bah.
(Catches herself before hanging up)

Oh, say -- Bill? Hang on a sec. I forgot to ask you--
...No, seriously, listen, you will know the answer to this. So, now, if you --if you are born in Arkansas- and you get married in Arkansas -- but then, you move to Texas, and you get a divorce? Are you still brother

and sister? *(She hangs up and does a ridiculous little dance, whistles, phone rings)*

ANN

Yeah? Suzanne? My Stars! *(Amazed)* Hi. So, look, this speech is in good enough shape-- Ima switch it to Brandeis and we'll save the first amendment stuff for NPR. Better for them anyway. *(She picks up speech, sits to mark it with a pencil)*
...But the way we close is too dry, too abstract. And it is so dark. I'm afraid those poor people in Boston are just gonna slash their wrists... yeah- no, jus' think of a good joke or something I can stick in there.

But, now-- the ending, when we're talking about Katrina and how here a year later nothing has happened-- I want to change the focus from us complaining about the government, to looking at our part in it. *(She gets up, striding as she presents her ideas)* I mean we all do this, ya know? -We all whine and complain, "the government is horrible- they don't do this!" -'n' "they don't do that!" Hell, I complain about "they,"-and I was a governor! So use the line "we hafta stop whining and start participating." *(Low)* My lord, Suzanne, half the country doesn't even vote!

OK! Start with this. Say- "Think- think of all those people from around the globe, who leave everything behind, their homelands, their families, all they have-- to come to our country, where they can vote." Put that in. Then jump to something like - ahhh- *(The light isolates her, the skyline dims)* Let's look at the big picture. What will they say of our time? What will they say of us?- That here-- in the land of the free, voting- fell out of fashion? *(She hits speaker button, puts receiver in the cradle, and leans on the table)*

'N' listen, it's not that good things always happen
when good people vote-- But it is darn sure true that
bad things happen when they don't vote. *(Head coming
up)* And voting is the least of it.

> *And now ANN pushes away from
> the table which drops away,
> and turns front to standing
> and into the full out speech.*

I don't understand people who turn their back on it
all-- because the government is the most pervasive
institution in our lives-- And if you don't
participate, you are letting other people make some big
old decisions for you.

Ima cut to the chase. The Government isn't "they!" The
government- is you! It is me, it is us! --And sometimes
"us," not at our very best. Public Servants work for
you-- *(Her 'trumpet voice' begins)* You have the power
to call 'em out, and call 'em down. YOU hire 'em, you
can fire 'em! If they are racist, if they are sexist,
if they are wrong-- YOU- MUST- CALL 'EM OUT! *(Now she
becomes quiet, gentle, sly)*

And instead of complaining about "they", whyn't some a'you
infiltrate the enemy! *(Laughs)* Become one o' them- for real!

True public service requires a passion, and I know
there are always those few who have the heart for
it. Lotta you won't even contemplate it 'cause you
see politics as so dirty. Well, I wish you'd think
it over... especially you women. Hell - We've seen
far dirtier fights in the PTA, haven't we! And besides
which, the Nation needs you! *(Now she is mild)*

Simply viewed, while men are great fighters-- women have
a talent for bringing consensus. Ya know--? All those

hours at the dinner table, trying to make sure everyone
has their say and gets a piece of the pie, too.

For me, and a lot of public servants, --it is almost
a calling-- Not from "on high," -but from within...
that in our core, we feel we can make life better for
people, in a way beyond our own family.

But for all us citizens... Men and women- we're all in
this together. We should all pull together. That way--
maybe we've got a shot.

And anyway, why should your life be just about you?

> _The light blows up bright--!_
> _and almost out. In darkness,_
> _a column of down light, a_
> _sifting of silver dust falls._
> _ANN, now in shadow, stands_
> _looking off. A dim grainy_
> _B&W projection, a casket_
> _in procession- appears and_
> _quickly fades out. Ann walks_
> _to where the silver fell._
> _She's light and exuberant._

                    ANN

I never did get to give that speech! But you remember
what John Lennon sung to us about how life happens
while we're making other plans? My plans were pulled up
short with a turn in my health.

You know, just the word cancer is so potent, people
even look down when they say it...
So here was another battle in my life-- and I ain't
never run from a fight yet. I was gonna approach it the

way I did anything: "hit the gas."

'N' before you get some fancy idea I was a big hero
about it- lemme tell you, it's like that country song
about crying they usta play out at the skating rink
when I was a kid, "at midnight tears run into your
ears!" I am sure I cried my share- and then some!
Shoot, nobody wants to go. But you know what they say
about battles-- "You can't win 'em all!"

Now, this will sound funny t' y'all, coming from me,
but the memorials and the funeral that my old staff and
friends and family had about one day to pull together,
were just... so FABULOUS. I don't know how those guys
whipped up these coupla memorials out of plain air--
but there's President Clinton, speaking in the Capital
Rotunda, *(She looks up at the grandeur)* with me under
a flag for godssakes... I mean, it was like they were
planting a general or something!

And my God, this other deal, where Hillary Clinton
spoke, with thousands of people, and gospel singing,
and big speeches and stories-- and my granddaughter
Lily, so slender and tall, spoke at the end-- and was,
I have to admit it, entirely perfect.

There's a poem that long ago I had stumbled on, and
really 'loved- and I casually tossed it to Suzanne, and
said, "save this for me," you know? In case I needed it
for a funeral...
Of course, I wasn't thinking it'd be MINE!! And I
can't believe it, but not only did she save it, she
remembered where she put it! That Suzanne. She was too
shy to read it at the funeral, o' course, but Jane
wadn't, and Jane j's nailed it.
It has lines like- *(She remembers it readily)* "Call me by
my old familiar name." Love that. And- "Whatever we were

to each other, that we still are." And then- Oh, yeah-
(The podium has returned) "I am somewhere very near..."
Now, traditionally, you're supposed to close these
things with a pearl of wisdom, but what do I know? I
lived my life pell-mell, like anybody else! Oh, the
battles lost and won... Oh, the things I had to have!
Well, in the long haul, I wouldn't give you a nickel
for a cut glass bowl.

The here and now is all you have, and if you play it
right- it's all you need.

I wish for you...
That you would value the love of your family and
friends as if your life depends on it. Because it does.
That you'd take that chance on your dreams and bet on
yourself-- And just trust your wings will catch the wind.

After all-- You gotta go out on a limb, 'cause that's
where the fruit is.

Gosh, it is good to see you! It's good to be seen!
Well, thanks a lot- God Bless you- *(A quick
afterthought)* and Daddy, you were right, I was smart,
and I could do anything I wanted to!

And Mama... Well, --you got to meet the weatherman!

> *She exits upstage, nodding modestly,
> and, as she turns away, she makes
> a hat-tipping salute. Even if her
> audience is cheering, she is not
> certain she has done well.*
>
> *On the screen: a silvery black
> and white portrait, serene and
> lightly smiling.*

"Today we have a vision of a Texas where opportunity knows no race, no gender, no color – a glimpse of what can happen in government if we simply open the doors and let the people in."

Ann W. Richards
Inaugural Address
15 January 1991

In memoriam

September 1, 1933 — September 13, 2006

ACKNOWLEDGEMENTS

This play would not be possible without the generous support of the following people who served as the principal source of information and research.

Jane Hickie (Political Strategist and close friend), Mary Beth Rogers (Chief of Staff, Campaign Manager and friend), Claire Korioth (Gubernatorial Appointee and longtime friend), Cathy Bonner (Director of Department of Commerce and friend), Barbara Chapman (Executive Assistant, Austin), Sandra Castellanos (Executive Assistant, New York)

Additional credit and thanks:

Ave Bonar (Ann's Photographer), Bill Cryer (Press Secretary), Martha Smiley (UT Board of Regents), Suzanne Coleman (Speech Writer), David Talbot (General Council), Cecile Richards (Daughter and President of Planned Parenthood), Dan Richards (Son, Attorney), Clark Richards (Son, Attorney), Ellen Richards (Daughter), Lily Adams (Granddaughter), David Miller (Administration), Jaston Williams (Playwright, Actor and Supporter), Bud Shrake (Renowned Writer and longtime friend), Jennifer Treat (Head of Fundraising), Gail Huitt (life-long hair dresser), Wayne Slater (Journalist), Janet Allen (Administrative Aide), Chula Reynolds (Supporter and friend), Don Temples (Administrative Aide), Patrick Terry (Bluebonnet Club Administrator and whippersnapper in the day), Liz Smith (close personal friend in later years), Barry Bridges (DPS Security Officer), Maynon Laverne "M.L." Routt (personal housekeeper), Karen Knippa (massage therapist in her last years), Billy Rhea (DPS Security Officer), Evan Smith (then Editor of Texas Monthly), Ali James (Texas State Capital Curator), Mark Strama (Texas House of Representatives)

Other sources simply too numerous to mention.

All photos herein credited to Ave Bonar unless otherwise noted. Ave Bonar had the unique opportunities to photograph the 1990 Ann Richards campaign for Texas governor and then 20 years later to photograph the production of Holland Taylor's play, *Ann*. See more of her work at avebonarphotography.com.

Creative direction by Kevin Bailey, MB Artists.
Produced for publication by Amy S. Layton, Hook 'em Marketing.
Layout by Nancy Josephson, Design Farm.